EAR T

Climate Change

by Helen Orme

ticktock

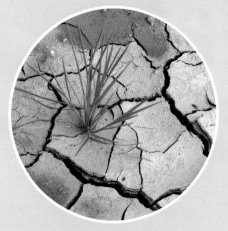

By Helen Orme
Series consultant: Terry Jennings
ticktock editor: Sophie Furse
ticktock designer: Hayley Terry
Picture research: Lizzie Knowles
With thanks to: Joe Harris, Mark Sachner and Claire Lucas

Copyright © ticktock Entertainment Ltd 2008
First published in Great Britain in 2008 by ticktock Media Ltd,
Unit 2, Orchard Business Centre, North Farm Road,
Tunbridge Wells, Kent, TN2 3XF

ISBN 978 1 84696 734 4 pbk
Printed in China

Picture credits
Age fotostock/ SuperStock: OFC, 20-21. Niclas Albinsson/ Jupiter Images: 4-5. John Armstrong Miller/ iStock: 13 inset.
Corbis/ Photolibrary Group: 6-7. iStock: 9, 32. Allan Ivy/ Alamy: 29b. Patricio Robles Gil/Sierra Madre/Minden
Pictures/FLPA: 15 (inset). Patricio Robles Gil/ FLPA: 14-15. Shutterstock: 2, 4l, 7t, 8, 9 inset, 10, 11, 12-13, 16, 17, 18-19,
19 inset, 22-23, 24 all, 25 all, 26, 27t, 27b, 28, 29c, 30, 31, 32, OBC.
Every effort has been made to trace the copyright holders, and we apologise in advance for any unintentional omissions.
We would be pleased to insert the appropriate acknowledgements in any subsequent edition of this publication.

CONTENTS

Words that appear **in bold** are explained in the glossary.

WHAT IS CLIMATE CHANGE?

Our weather is always changing! It can change from hour to hour, from day to day, and from season to season.

The average weather in a place over many years is called the **climate**. This can also change.

For example, about 1.8 million years ago, most of North America was covered in ice. This **ice age** lasted until 11,500 years ago. Then the climate slowly became warmer and the ice melted.

These slow changes have happened many times in Earth's history. Today, however, there is a problem. The climate is changing quickly, and scientists think it is because of the way people live today.

°C °F

50 — 120

40 — 100

30 — 80

20 — 60

10 — 40

0 — 32

-10 — -20

WHAT HAS CHANGED?

Climate changes that once took thousands of years may now take only a few hundred years. Some changes may be even faster. Changes that began about 100 years ago have speeded up in the last 50 years.

How is the climate changing? Temperatures are rising. Storms are becoming more frequent and more powerful. The warmer climate means that the **polar icecaps** and **glaciers** are melting.

Most scientists agree that these changes are caused by the way we live now.

The patterns of rainfall are changing. Some places are getting much less rain. Other places are getting much more rain.

BURNING FOSSIL FUELS

What is causing these changes to happen more quickly?

In the last fifty years, the number of cars, trucks, planes, and motorcycles that people use has gone up. People have also built many more factories and power stations.

Most of these are powered by burning **fossil fuels**. When fossil fuels are burnt, the carbon they contain is released as **carbon dioxide** gas.

Scientists believe that releasing more carbon dioxide gas is bad for the climate. It is making our planet warm up.

Today in the UK there are 27.8 million cars on the road. That's enough to fill a 52-lane motorway from London to Edinburgh.

FOSSIL FUELS

Coal, oil and gas are all
fossil fuels. They are made
from the remains of plants
and animals that died
millions of years ago.

GREENHOUSE GASES AT WORK

*The Sun warms the Earth. Then the Earth warms the layer of gases that surround the Earth. These gases are called the **atmosphere**.*

Some gases in the atmosphere, such as carbon dioxide, trap the Sun's heat – just like the glass in a gardener's greenhouse. They are known as **greenhouse gases**.

Without these gases, the world would be too cold for living things.

However, if we put more gases, such as carbon dioxide, into the atmosphere, too much heat will be trapped.

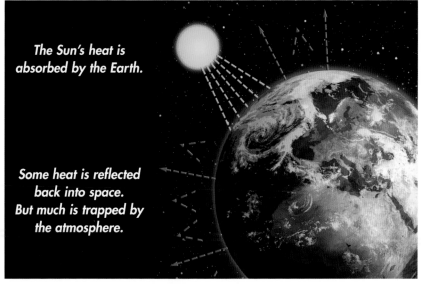

The Sun's heat is absorbed by the Earth.

Some heat is reflected back into space. But much is trapped by the atmosphere.

This shows how greenhouse gases trap heat inside Earth's atmosphere. If too many of these gases are trapped, the temperature could become too warm.

Earth's temperature now is just right to support all the plant, animal and human life that exists. Heat trapped within the atmosphere could make the world warmer. This would affect all life, and could put many species of plants and animals in danger.

Warmer temperatures would mean waterholes could dry up. This would leave many animals like this African elephant in need of water.

GLOBAL WARMING

*We need some greenhouse gases in our atmosphere, but too much of them will cause **global warming**. However, this doesn't mean there will be sunnier weather.*

In some places, global warming will be mild and just make summers hotter and winters less cold. But it could also cause extreme **heat waves.**

Global warming could affect wind patterns in the atmosphere and make storms more severe.

These changes will have a big effect on people's lives.

More rainfall could mean more flooding from hurricanes and other violent storms.

MELTING ICE

One effect of a warmer world is that ice on mountains and in the Arctic and Antarctic will melt! Changes are already happening.

In the Arctic a large area of the ocean is frozen all the year. This is called the 'icecap'. In winter, the ocean around the icecap freezes, too. The amount of ocean that freezes is getting smaller each year.

If the ice and snow on land in the Arctic and Antarctic melts, sea levels will rise. This will cause flooding to many places around the world.

Amount of frozen Ocean in 1981.

Frozen Arctic Ocean

Amount of frozen Ocean in 2005.

Icecap

HUNTING FOR SEALS

Polar bears hunt seals on the frozen Arctic Ocean during the autumn, winter, and spring. Each year, the sea ice melts earlier and freezes later. The bears' hunting season is getting shorter, making it hard for them to catch enough food to survive.

When Hurricane Katrina hit New Orleans in 2005, many of the levees (protective banks) broke and the city was flooded.

RISING SEA LEVELS

Melting ice and snow is the best-known cause of rising sea levels. There is however another factor that could raise the levels of the oceans and seas.

When water warms up, it expands (gets bigger). Higher temperatures will warm the oceans and seas. As the water expands, sea levels will rise even more.

Low-lying coastal cities, such as London, New York, and New Orleans, could be flooded!

The Maldives are islands in the Indian Ocean. Many of the islands are only a metre above sea level. Rising sea levels means these islands will be underwater in the next 100 years.

DROUGHTS AND DESERTS

Scientists believe that, because of global warming, some places will have less rainfall in the future. They also believe warmer temperatures may dry up water on land. Together these could lead to **droughts.**

A drought is a long period of time with little or no rainfall.

During a drought, the soil becomes dry and cracked. Only a few plants can survive. Without plants to nourish the soil and help keep it damp, the land may be damaged forever.

Over time, damaged land could even become a **desert**.

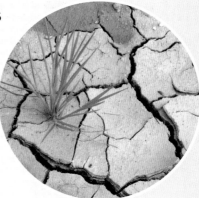

Grazing animals on dry, damaged land makes the plant life disappear even faster.

Herding animals in one of the dry, desert areas of the Atlas Mountains in Morocco.

19

RAINFORESTS HELP FIGHT GREENHOUSE GASES

The good news is that there are things we can do to slow down climate change.

Trees and other plants absorb carbon dioxide, and release **oxygen**. This stops greenhouse gases building up in the atmosphere where they cause global warming.

The Earth's **rainforests** contain millions of trees and plants.

However, too many rainforest trees are now being cut down for lumber or to make space for growing crops.

Saving the rainforests is a major way we can help slow down climate change.

This map shows the Earth's major rainforests in dark green.

This Scarlet Macaw parrot lives in the warm, wet environment of the Amazon rainforest. So much of their habitat has been destroyed that they are now in danger of becoming extinct.

NATURE AND HUMANS WORKING TOGETHER

It's not too late to help our planet if humans and nature work together.

Soil that has been badly damaged by drought can recover in time. Just a small amount of rain will allow plants to begin to grow. If people stop using the land, nature will reclaim it.

Allowing trees, especially rainforest trees, to grow will help to reduce the amount of carbon dioxide in the air.

In the future, we must find ways to avoid burning so much fossil fuel. This will reduce the amount of carbon dioxide in the atmosphere and slow down global warming.

Wildflowers in the Joshua Tree National Park, USA. Spring rains help the flowers bloom throughout this desert.

MAKING ELECTRICITY

Today, most of the electricity we use comes from power stations that burn fossil fuels. In the future, we need to find different ways to produce electricity that don't create greenhouse gases. Here are some good and bad points of a few of the different ways to make power.

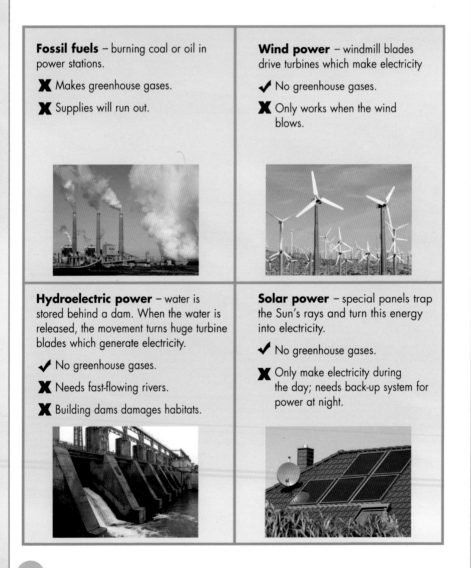

Fossil fuels – burning coal or oil in power stations.

✘ Makes greenhouse gases.

✘ Supplies will run out.

Wind power – windmill blades drive turbines which make electricity

✔ No greenhouse gases.

✘ Only works when the wind blows.

Hydroelectric power – water is stored behind a dam. When the water is released, the movement turns huge turbine blades which generate electricity.

✔ No greenhouse gases.

✘ Needs fast-flowing rivers.

✘ Building dams damages habitats.

Solar power – special panels trap the Sun's rays and turn this energy into electricity.

✔ No greenhouse gases.

✘ Only make electricity during the day; needs back-up system for power at night.

USE LESS ELECTRICITY

One way we can make a difference to the climate is to use less electricity.

A low-energy light bulb.

- Use energy saving light bulbs.

- Don't leave the TV or your computer on stand-by – turn it off!

- Turn the heating down and put a thick sweater on instead!

- Draw your curtains. Even double-glazed windows let a lot of heat leak outside.

- Go solar! Schools and factories work mainly in the day. If they use solar panels to generate electricity it will reduce the amount of energy they need to get from power stations.

Schools only need energy during the day.

Saving water and electricity.

- Take showers instead of baths. Showers use less water than baths. This means less water needs to be heated up which saves electricity.

CHANGE THE WAY YOU TRAVEL

We love to travel around in cars and planes, but they both burn fossil fuels. Planes produce more carbon dioxide than any other form of transport. They produce it high in the atmosphere, where it can do the most damage.

Cycling holidays are becoming more popular.

• Walk or cycle instead of going by car.

• Use buses and trains. When lots of people travel together in one vehicle, fewer greenhouse gases are produced per person.

• Use a car that is powered by an electric battery. Some greenhouse gases are produced by creating the electricity for the battery, but fewer than a petrol-powered car produces.

• Hybrid cars are powered by electric batteries and petrol. Hybrid cars can switch from their petrol-powered engines to electric batteries when the car is not moving. This reduces the amount of greenhouse gases they produce.

• Take holidays closer to home so you don't need to fly. Or take shorter flights so airlines can use smaller, low-flying planes that produce less greenhouse gases.

TREES ARE OUR FRIENDS!

• Trees soak up carbon dioxide from the atmosphere. This helps to reduce global warming.

• Trees help fight the damage caused by heavy rains and flooding. Like all plants, their roots help hold down the soil and keep it from washing away.

Tree roots help keep soil in place.

HELPING FORESTS

• Sadly, at the moment we are not treating our forests very well. We cut down trees for wood and to make paper.

• Forests are also cut down to clear land for roads, homes and to grow crops.

MADE OF
100%
RECYCLED
PAPER

• We can help the forests by recycling paper and only buying recycled paper products.

• Only buy wooden items made from trees that have been specially planted for that purpose. Ask in the shop if they know where the wood comes from.

• We can also encourage people who live in forested areas to find other ways of making a living, and to learn how to reuse land that has already been cleared.

27

COPING WITH CLIMATE CHANGE WHERE WE LIVE

We won't be able to stop all the effects of climate change. So in the future we will have to find ways to deal with changes in our climate.

We will need to protect ourselves from flooding.

• We can build flood barriers, such as the Thames Barrier in London and improved levees (protective banks) in New Orleans, USA.

The Thames Barrier in London, UK.

We will also need to find ways to cope with hotter temperatures.

• Many modern buildings use air-conditioning to keep cool, but this uses a lot of electricity. Instead of air-conditioning, we can wear loose, light clothing and drink plenty of water to keep cool.

• Keeping the curtains closed will help to keep rooms cool during the heat of the day, too.

FLOODING CASE STUDY - BANGLADESH

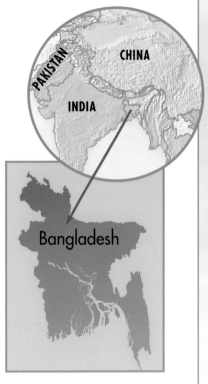

Bangladesh

• Bangladesh, in Asia, is not very high above sea level. Most of its land is at the mouths of three large rivers.

• Some areas in Bangladesh are regularly flooded either by the sea, or by rivers that overflow after heavy rain.

• Bangladesh also suffers fierce tropical storms that bring high winds and lots of rain.

• Many Bangladeshi people are very poor. They lose everything if their homes are flooded. One answer is to build homes up on platforms that are safe from flooding.

• The walls of the house below are made out of bamboo. This is cheap to replace.

This house is easy for people to rebuild themselves if it is damaged by floods.

• Re-use and recycle! It takes huge amounts of energy to make new glass and plastic bottles or metal cans. Much less energy is needed to make bottles and cans from old recycled material.

• Keep a climate diary at your school. Write down the weather conditions for every day of the year. Add up the number of sunny, rainy, or snowy days, and put the totals in the diary. Future students can look at your diary and see what climate changes have occurred in your neighbourhood.

• Do an energy check on your school as a project. How good is your school at turning off lights in rooms that aren't being used? How about computers on standby? Are rooms too hot in the winter? How many ways can you come up with to save energy?

Visit these websites for more information and to find out how you can help stop climate change.

BBC: www.bbc.co.uk/sn/hottopics/climatechange

World Wildlife Fund International: www.wwf.org

GLOSSARY

atmosphere The air, and gases that surround our planet.

carbon dioxide A greenhouse gas given off when things decay or are burnt.

climate Patterns of weather over a long period of time.

desert Dry land with few plants and little rainfall. Deserts are often covered in sand.

drought A long period of time with little or no rainfall, or less rainfall than usual.

fossil fuels Fuels such as coal, oil and gas made from the remains of plants and animals that died millions of years ago.

glaciers Huge, slow-moving rivers of ice, often about 30 metres thick. Glaciers move slowly down a slope or valley.

global warming The warming of the Earth's air and oceans because of a build-up of greenhouse gases in the atmosphere.

greenhouse gases Gases, such as carbon dioxide, that trap warm air in the atmosphere so it cannot escape into space.

heat waves Periods of unusually hot weather.

ice age A period of time when massive sheets of ice, or glaciers, covered large areas of the Earth.

oxygen A gas in the Earth's atmosphere. Humans and almost all other living things need oxygen to breathe.

polar icecaps Large areas of permanently frozen ice in the Arctic Ocean (North Pole) and at Antarctica (South Pole).

rainforests Huge forests of tall trees. Rainforests are normally warm and have lots of rain.

INDEX